Laravel Basics

Creating Web Apps. It's Simple.

Table of Contents

Introduction

Laravel is a PHP framework which helps in the development of web apps. Compared to CodeIgnitor, Laravel is more advanced. Currently, Laravel is at version 5.3, and this version has brought in a number of changes and improvements to the Laravel framework. The framework has been designed so as to help you develop web apps in an easier and rapid style. You can also use this framework for performing large-scale work. This book guides you on how to use the Laravel framework. Enjoy reading!

Chapter 1- What is Laravel?

Laravel is a framework for the development of web applications, and it has an expressive and elegant syntax. It tries to make the process of development of web applications easier by making common tasks such as routing, authentication, caching, and sessions easy. The application functionality is maintained, but the development process is made very easy.

You can easily access Laravel, and it provides you with some of the most powerful tools which can help in the development of large and robust applications. Currently, the latest version of Laravel is 5.3, and this has made some improvements to version 5.2. It comes with a notification system which is based on drivers, robust realtime support via Laravel Scout, support for Webpack via Laravel Elixir, objects which are mailable, closure based console commands, convenient helpers for the storage of files which are uploaded, single-action controllers and POPO, and improved scaffolding on the default frontend.

Chapter 2- Notifications

Laravel Notifications provide us with a simple and expressive Application Programming Interface (API) which we can use to send notifications across a wide range of delivery channels such as Slack, email, SMS, and others. As anxample, you can create a invoice showing a payment for an invoice and then deliver that notification via SMS or email. You can then use a very simple method so as to relay the notification. This is shown below:

$user->notify(new InvoicePaid($invoice));

The "user" is the one to which the notification is to be sent. Note the use of the method named "notify" so as to send the notification to the user. The attribute "$invoice" should specify the invoice which has been paid. Note that Laravel 5.3 has introduced numerous community-written drivers which support the use of notifications.

Creating Notifications

In Laravel, the representation of notifications is done with a single class, and this is typically stored in the directory "app/Notifications." In some cases, you may not find the directory in your system, but you don't have to worry, as it will be automatically created   once you execute the Artisan command "make:notification."

Once the above command is executed, a fresh notification class is created and placed in the directory "make:notification." Note that each notification class should have the "via" class and a number of methods for building messages. These methods are responsible for converting the notification into a message so that it can be sent over the channel.

Sending Notifications

Using Notifiable Trait

There are two ways for us to send notifications in Laravel. In the first method, we can use the "notify" method of the "Notifiable" trait or the Notification façade. The Notifiable trait is used by the App\Use model, which is the default model, It has only a single method, that is, "notify," which we can use for the purpose of sending notifications. The method should receive a notification instance as shown below:

use App\Notifications\InvoicePaid;

$user->notify(new InvoicePaid($invoice));

Note that in the above example, we have used the "new" keyword for creation of the instance of notification, and we have named it "InvoicePaid."

Notification Façade

We can also use the Notification Façade so as to send notifications. This is normally used when we need to send the notifications to a variety of notifiable entities, such as a collection of users.

For you to use the façade for sending notifications, all the notification entities have to be passed together with the notification instance via the "send" method. This is shown below:

Notification::send($users, new InvoicePaid($invoice));

In the above case, "send" is the method, "users" represents the users to receive the notification, while "InvoicePaid" is the notification instance.

Specification of Delivery Channels

Each notification class has the "via" method for determination of the channels through which the notification will be delivered. Notifications can be sent on channels such as mail, broadcast, nexmo, database, and slack.

The "via" method should receive the "$notifiable" instance, and this should be the class instance to which your notification is being sent. You may use the "$notifiable" for the determination of the channels to which your notification will be delivered to:

```
/**
 * Getting the delivery channels for the notification.
 *
 * @param mixed $notifiable
 * @return array
 */
public function via($notifiable)
{
    return $notifiable->prefers_sms ? ['nexmo'] : ['mail', 'database'];
}
```

How to Queue Notifications

The process of sending a notification can be tedious, and especially in cases where an external API call has to be made for the notification to be delivered. If you need to speed the response time of the app, you can let your notification to be queued (lined up in the order to be sent) by use of "ShouldQueue" interface and the "Queueable" trait to the class. The interface and the trait are readily imported for the notifications generated by the use of "make:notification," meaning that they should be immediately added to the notification class. This is shown below:

```php
<?php

namespace App\Notifications;

use Illuminate\Notifications\Notification;
use Illuminate\Bus\Queueable;
use Illuminate\Contracts\Queue\ShouldQueue;

class InvoicePaid extends Notification implements ShouldQueue
{
    use Queueable;

    // ...
}
```

After the interface "ShouldQueue" has been added to the notification, and the notification can then be sent normally. That is what we have done in the above example. Laravel will detect the "ShouldQueue" interface in the class, and the notification delivery will be automatically queued. This is shown below:

```php
$user->notify(new InvoicePaid($invoice));
```

Sometimes, you may need to delay the delivery of the notification. In such a case, the "delay" method has to be chained to the instantiation of the notification. This is shown below:

```php
$when = Carbon::now()->addMinutes(5);

$user->notify((new InvoicePaid($invoice))->delay($when));
```

The instantiation of the notification in the above example happens in the second line, and it has been done by the use of the "new" keyword. That is where the "delay" method has been added or chained. In the method, the delay variable has been named "when," and we want to delay the notification for 5 minutes. This variable "when" has been called or passed as an argument in the "delay" method in the second line. Note that we have used the "addMinutes" method to add the minutes as shown in the first line.

Mail Notifications

If it is possible for a notification to be sent via email, then the method "toMail" has to be specified in the notification class. The method will get the "$notifiable" entity, and an instance of "Illuminate\Notifications\Messages\MailMessage" will be returned. The mail messages or notifications can have both text and a "call to action." Consider the example given below:

```
/**
 * Getting the representation of the notification in mail.
 *
 * @param  mixed  $notifiable
 * @return \Illuminate\Notifications\Messages\MailMessage
 */
public function toMail($notifiable)
{
    $url = url('/invoice/'.$this->invoice->id);

    return (new MailMessage)
        ->line('You have received payment for one of your invoices!')

        ->action('View Invoice', $url)
        ->line('Continue using our app. Thank you!');
}
```

Note that the "$this->invoice->id" has been used in the "message" method. Any data needed by the notification may be passed into the constructor of the message so as to generate the message. In the example, two lines of text and a call to action have been specified. Note that the call to action has been specified by the use of "action." The "$url" parameter will show a link leading to the invoice and once clicked, the user will view the invoice. The URL was specified in the line "**$url = url('/invoice/'.$this->invoice->id);**" and the "id" parameter refers to the unique id of the invoice.

The methods used above are provided by the class "MailMessage," and they make it easy and fast for us to format the small transactional emails. The mail channel will be tasked with the translation and formatting of the message components into a good and responsive HTML email template.

Customization of the Recipient

Whenever a notification is to be sent via the "mail" channel, the notification system will have to look for the "email" property on the notifiable entity. The email address to deliver the notification can be customized by the use of the "routeNotificationForMail" method on your entity.

This is shown below:

```php
<?php

namespace App;

use Illuminate\Foundation\Auth\User as Authenticatable;

use Illuminate\Notifications\Notifiable;

class User extends Authenticatable
{
```

```
use Notifiable;

/**
 * Routing the notifications for our mail channel.
 *
 * @return string
 */
public function routeNotificationForMail()
{
    return $this->email_address;
}
}
```

Note that in the above example, the parameter **"email_address"** should be replaced with the email address which is to be used for the delivery of the notification. Note how this has been defined within the **"routeNotificationForMail()"** method.

Customization of the Subject

The default setting is that the subject of the email is the name of the notification which has been formatted to the title case. This means that if you use the name "InvoiceReceived" as the notification name, then the subject name will be "Invoice Received." However, you may not be interested in this, but instead, you may need to   explicitly specify the subject when constructing the message. This can be done by the use of the "subject" method as shown below:

```
/**
 * Obtain the representation of the notification in mail.
 *
 * @param  mixed  $notifiable
 * @return \Illuminate\Notifications\Messages\MailMessage
 */
public function toMail($notifiable)
{
```

```
    return (new MailMessage)
        ->subject('Subject of the Notification')
        ->line('...');
}
```

Note that the methods "subject" and "line" have been used within the instantiation of "MailMessage." The "subject" method specifies the subject of the message, while the "line" method specifies some text. Feel free to add some text to the method.

Customization of the Template

The template which is being used by the mail notifications can be modified once we publish the package resources of the notification. We can run the command given below, and the notification template for the mail will be found in the "resources/views/vendor/notifications" directory. Here is the command:

php artisan vendor:publish --tag laravel-notifications

Let us explore how the customization can be done.

Error Messages

Sometimes, errors do occur and we can use notifications to inform the user about the same. A mail message can be designated to report an error by calling the "error" method when we are building the message.
 Once you use this method in your message, then your "call to action" button will have a red color, but its normal color is blue. Consider the following example:

```
/**
 * Obtain the notification presentation in mail form.
 *
 * @param  mixed  $notifiable
 * @return \Illuminate\Notifications\Message
 */
public function toMail($notifiable)
{
    return (new MailMessage)
        ->error()
        ->subject('Subject of the Notification')
        ->line('...');
}
```

As shown in the above code, the "error()" method has no parameter, but Laravel will understand what it means, and the notification will be designated as an error.

Database Notifications

This model of notification works by storing the notification data in a table of a database. The table stores information related to the type of the notification, and some JSON data which is tasked with description of the notification.

The table can be queried so as to show the data about the notification on the interface of the application. However, you should begin by creating a database table which will be tasked with holding the notifications. The "notifications:table" command can be used for the generation of a migration with a proper table schema. This is shown below:

php artisan notifications:table
php artisan migrate
How to Format the Database Notifications

If a notification can be stored in a database table, the method "toArray" or "toDatabase" can be defined on the notification class. The method will then get an entity of the type "$notifiable" and a plain PHP array will be returned. The array to be returned will have to be encoded in the JSON format, and then it will be kept in the "data" column in the "notifications" table.

The following example demonstrates how the "toArray" method can be used:

```
/**
 * Get the notification represented as an array.
 *
 * @param mixed $notifiable
 * @return array
 */
```

```
public function toArray($notifiable)
{
  return [
    'invoice_id' => $this->invoice->id,
    'amount' => $this->invoice->amount,
  ];
}
```

You should note that the "toArray" method is used by the broadcast channel for determination of the data which is to be broadcast to the JavaScript client. The above code will give us the invoice id and its amount paid.

How to Access the Notifications

Since the notifications are stored in a database table, we have to come up with an appropriate mechanism for accessing them from the notifiable entities.
The trait "Illuminate\Notifications\Notifiable" has a "notifications" relationship which will return the notification for the entity. When we need to fetch the notification, the method can be accessed in the normal way. The default setting is that the "created_at" will sort the notifications. This is shown below:

```
$user = App\User::find(1);
foreach ($user->notifications as $notification) {
  echo $notification->type;
}
```

The above code should give you all the notifications for all users. However, sometimes, you may need to get only the unread notifications, and this can be done by the use of the "unreadNotifications" relationship. The notifications will also be sorted by use of the "created_at" timestamp. This is shown below:

```
$user = App\User::find(1);
```

```
foreach            ($user->unreadNotifications        as
$notification) {

    echo $notification->type;
}
```

In the second line of the above code, we have used the variable "notification" to represent the unread notifications. This has been implemented by the use of the "unreadNotifications" function. We can then echo this variable as shown in the last line, and we will get all the unread notifications.

Marking the Read Notifications

Once the user has viewed a notification, it should be marked as read. The "Illuminate\Notifications\Notifiable" trait has a method named "markAsRead" which will update the method named "read_at" on the database record of the notification. This is shown below:

```
$user = App\User::find(1);
```

```
foreach ($user->notifications as $notification) {
    $notification->markAsRead();
}
```

In the second of the above code, the variable "notification" has been used to represent all the notifications which the user has read. In the last line of the code, we have used the "markAsRead()" method so as to mark these as read.

The problem with the above code is that we will have to loop over all our notifications. We can avoid this by using the method "markAsRead" directly on the collection of notifications. This can be done as follows:

```
$user->notifications->markAsRead();
```

A mass update query can also be used for marking all the notifications as read with no need for us to retrieve them from the database. This is shown below:

$user = App\User::find(1);

**$user->notifications()->update(['read_at'   =>
Carbon::now()]);**

Note that we have used the "update" query, which is a very common database operation. The column named "read_at" will be updated so as to show that all the notifications have been read. Note that we have used the "now()" method. This means that the timestamp at which the notifications were read will be set to the time at which you executed the above program.

The "delete" operation or query is also common in the database operations. This can be used in Laravel for the deletion of the notifications from the database. This is shown below:

$user->notifications()->delete();

Broadcast Notifications

For you to broadcast your notifications, you should configure and familiarize yourself with the event broadcasting services of Laravel. With event broadcasting, we can react to the Laravel events which are fired from the server-side on the JavaScript client.

How to Format Broadcast Notifications

The "broadcast" channel will use the event broadcasting services of Laravel so as to allow the JavaScript client to fetch or get the notifications in a real time manner.

If the notification is in support of broadcasting, then it will be good for you to define the "toArray" or the "toBroadcast" method on your notification class. The method will get a "$notifiable" entity, and a plain PHP array will be returned. The array will be in JSON format and broadcast to the JavaScript client. Consider the following example, which used the "toArray" method:

```php
/**
 * Get the notification represented as an array.
 *
 * @param  mixed  $notifiable
 * @return array
 */
public function toArray($notifiable)
{
    return [
        'invoice_id' => $this->invoice->id,
        'amount' => $this->invoice->amount,
    ];
}
```

The invoice will then be represented in an array format. The "toArray" method has helped us implement this.

How to Listen to the Notifications

Broadcasting of notifications is done on a private channel by use of the convention "{notifiable}.{id}." This means that if a notification with an id of 2 is to be transmitted via the "App\User" private channel, then the notification will be broadcast on the private channel named "App.User.2." By use of the Laravel echo, one can easily listen for the notifications on the channel by use of the helper method named "notification." This is shown below:

```javascript
Echo.private('App.User.' + userId)
    .notification((notification) => {
        console.log(notification.type);
```

```
});
```

We have used the "notification" helper method so as to listen to the notification on the channel. We have then called the "type" method so as to print the type of the notification we have.

SMS Notifications

Laravel relies on Nexmo for the purpose of sending SMS notifications. For this to be done, you should first install the nexmo/client composer package and then perform some additional configurations on the PHP configuration file named "config/services.php." The following is an example configuration which you can use so as to get started:

```
'nexmo' => [
   'key' => env('NEXMO_KEY'),
   'secret' => env('NEXMO_SECRET'),
   'sms_from' => '72562674536',
],
```

The field "sms_from" just specifies the number from which the SMS will be sent. The Nexmo control panel can let you create a phone number for your application, so go ahead and do so.

How to Format the SMS Notification

If a notification can be sent as an SMS, then you have to define the method "toNexmo" in the class for the notification. The method will receive the entity "$notifiable," and the instance "Illuminate\Notifications\Messages\NexmoMessage" will be returned. This is shown below:

```
/**
 * Get the notification represented in Nexmo / SMS.
 *
 * @param  mixed  $notifiable
 * @return NexmoMessage
 */
```

```
public function toNexmo($notifiable)
{
   return (new NexmoMessage)
        ->content('Add the content for the message
here');

}
```

Note that the message itself has been added within the instantiation of NexmoMessage by use of the "content" method.

How to Customize the "From" Number

If you are in need of sending the notification from some phone number which is not the same as the one specified in "config/services.php," then you should use the "from" method within an instance of the "NexmoMessage." This is shown below:

```
/**
 * Get the notification represented in Nexmo / SMS.
 *
 * @param  mixed  $notifiable
 * @return NexmoMessage
 */
public function toNexmo($notifiable)
{
   return (new NexmoMessage)
        ->content('Add the message content here')
        ->from('72562674536');
}
```

Routing SMS Notification

When you are to send the notification via the "nexmo" channel, the system will automatically look for the phone number in the "phone_number" attribute of the notifiable entity. If you need to customize the phone number to which the notification is to be delivered, the method "routeNotificationForNexmo" has to be defined on the entity. This is shown below:

```php
<?php

namespace App;
use           Illuminate\Foundation\Auth\User           as
Authenticatable;

use Illuminate\Notifications\Notifiable;
class User extends Authenticatable
{
    use Notifiable;

    /**
     * Routing the notifications for Nexmo channel.
     *
     * @return string
     */
    public function routeNotificationForNexmo()
    {
        return $this->phone;
    }
}
```

Slack Notifications

For you to be able to send notifications via slack, you should first install a library named "Guzzle HTTP" via Composer. This can be done as follows:

composer require guzzlehttp/guzzle

Note that we have used the "require" command for installation of the library.
You should also configure the Incoming Webhook integration for the slack team. The integration will give you a URL to use for routing the slack notifications.

How to Format Slack Notifications

If it is possible for a notification to be sent as a Slack message, the "toSlack" method should be defined on the notification class. The method will return the "$notifiable" entity and then return an instance of "Illuminate\Notifications\Messages\SlackMessage." Slack messages may have text and some attachments for formatting an array of fields. Consider the example given below:

```
/**
 * Get the notification represented as a Slack.
 *
 * @param mixed $notifiable
 * @return SlackMessage
 */
public function toSlack($notifiable)
{
    return (new SlackMessage)
            ->content('Good news. Your invoice has been paid!');

}
```

As shown in the above code, the instantiation of the "SlackMessage" has been done within the "toSlack()" method by use of the "new" keyword.

Attachments in Slack

Attachments can also be added to slack messages. These provide us with richer formatting options compared to the simple text messages. We need to create an example in which an error notification will be sent for an exception which has occurred in the application. A link will be provided, and this will lead to more details regarding the exception. Here is the code for this:

```
/**
```

```
* Get the notification represented as a Slack.
*
* @param  mixed  $notifiable
* @return SlackMessage
*/
public function toSlack($notifiable)
{
    $url = url('/exceptions/'.$this->exception->id);

    return (new SlackMessage)
            ->error()
            ->content('Something wrong has happened!')
            ->attachment(function ($attachment) use ($url) {

                $attachment->title('Exception: File was Not Found', $url)

                        ->content('File [image.jpg] was not found.');
            });
}
```

The code will raise an exception once it has been executed. This is because the file specified was not found. We have used the "$url" variable so that the text 'Exception: File was Not Found' will be clickable and lead to more information regarding the exception.

With attachments, one can also specify some data which is to be sent to a user and then be presented in a table format. The following example demonstrated how this can be done:

```
/**
* Get the notification represented as a Slack.
*
* @param  mixed  $notifiable
* @return SlackMessage
*/
```

```php
public function toSlack($notifiable)
{
    $url = url('/invoices/'.$this->invoice->id);

    return (new SlackMessage)
            ->success()
            ->content('Your invoice has been paid!')
            ->attachment(function    ($attachment)    use
($url) {

            $attachment->title('Invoice 1445', $url)
                ->fields([
                    'Title' => 'Travelling Expenses',
                    'Amount' => '$5,678',
                    'Via' => 'Visa Card',
                    'Was Overdue' => ':-1:',
                ]);
        });
}
```

The fields specified in the field part, that is, Title, Amount, Via, and Was Overdue, will be organized into a table.

Notification Events

After a notification has been sent, the notification system will fire the "Illuminate\Notifications\Events\NotificationSent" event. This should have the "notifiable" entity and the instance of the notification itself.

Listeners for an event can be registered in the "EventServiceProvider," as shown below:

```
/**
 * The mapping of the event listener for the application.
 *
 * @var array
 */
protected $listen = [
    'Illuminate\Notifications\Events\NotificationSent' => [

        'App\Listeners\LogNotification',
    ],
];
```

Once the listener has been registered in the "EventServiceProvider," the artisan command named "event:generate" can be used for the generation of the listener classes.

In the event listener, one can access the properties notifiable, notification, and channel on the event so as to learn about the notification or the notification recipient. This is shown below:

```
/**
 * Handling the event.
 *
 * @param NotificationSent $event
 * @return void
 */
```

```php
public function handle(NotificationSent $event)
{
    // $event->channel
    // $event->notifiable
    // $event->notification
}
```

Custom Channels

Laravel comes with a number of communication channels, but you may need to write your own drivers so that the notifications can be delivered via other channels. To demonstrate this, define a class with the name "send." Two arguments are to be passed to this method, that is, "$notifiable" and "$notification."

This is shown below:

```php
<?php

namespace App\Channels;

use Illuminate\Notifications\Notification;

class VoiceChannel
{
    /**
     * Sending the notification.
     *
     * @param  mixed  $notifiable
     * @param  \Illuminate\Notifications\Notification $notification
     *
     * @return void
     */
    public function send($notifiable, Notification $notification)

    {
```

```
    $message = $notification->toVoice($notifiable);

    // Send the notification to instance of the
$notifiable...

  }
}
```

The line " **$message = $notification->toVoice($notifiable);**" has implemented the sending of the notification to the instance of the "$notifiable" entity. The use of the "toVoice" method has helped us define the voice channel.

After definition of the notification channel, one may return the name of the class from the "via" method of one of the notifications. This is shown below:

```php
<?php
use Illuminate\Bus\Queueable;
use App\Channels\Messages\VoiceMessage;
use App\Channels\VoiceChannel;
use Illuminate\Notifications\Notification;
namespace App\Notifications;
use Illuminate\Contracts\Queue\ShouldQueue;

class InvoicePaid extends Notification
{
  use Queueable;

  /**
   * Get the channels for notification.
   *
   * @param  mixed  $notifiable
   * @return array|string
   */
  public function via($notifiable)
  {
    return [VoiceChannel::class];
```

```php
    }
    /**
     * Get the notification represented in voice.
     *
     * @param  mixed  $notifiable
     * @return VoiceMessage
     */
    public function toVoice($notifiable)
    {
        // ...
    }
}
```

Chapter 3- Event/ WebSockets Broadcasting

This feature was already available in Laravel before the release of version 5.3, but this version has improved it.

The entire event broadcasting configuration for the application has been stored in the configuration file named "config/broadcasting.php." There are several broadcast drivers which are supported in Laravel, such as Pusher, Log, and Redis which are in support of both debugging and local development. A null driver also exists, and this allows us to completely disable broadcasting.

Drivers

Pusher

If the events are to be broadcast via Pusher, one has to install the Pusher PHP SDK by use of the composer package manager. The following command can be used for this:

composer require pusher/pusher-php-server

After that, you should go ahead and configure the details for the Pusher in the file named "config/broadcasting.php," which is a configuration file.

When you are using the Laravel Echo and Pusher, you have to specify the Pusher as the desired broadcaster during the instantiation of the Echo instance. This is shown below:

import Echo from "laravel-echo"

```
window.Echo = new Echo({
    broadcaster: 'pusher',
    key: 'the-pusher-key'
});
```

The specification of this has been done in the line "broadcaster: 'pusher',."

Redis

If you need to use the Redis broadcaster, then you have to install the Predis library. The following command can help:

composer require predis/predis

The messages will be broadcast by use of the feature named "Redis' pub / sub." However, this has to be paired with a Websocket server capable of receiving messages from Redis and then broadcasting them to the Wbsocket channels.

Once an event has been published by the Websocket broadcaster, it has to be published on the channel names specified by the event, and the payload will be a string encoded in JSON having the name of the event, the data payload, and then the user who has generated the socket ID for the event.

Socket.IO

If the Redis broadcaster is to be paired with the Socket.IO server, then the JavaScript Client Library named Socket.IO has to be included in the head HTML element of the application. This is shown below:

```
<script src="https://cdn.socket.io/socket.io-1.4.5.js"></script>
```

You then instantiate the Echo with a "socket.io" connector and the "host." The following demonstrates how this can be done:

```
import Echo from "laravel-echo"

window.Echo = new Echo({
    broadcaster: 'socket.io',
    host: 'http://app.dev:6001'
});
```

The example demonstrates how the Echo can be instantiated when the application is running on the app.dev domain. The socket server is also running on the same domain.

Note that before you can broadcast events, you have to configure and then run some queue listener. Event broadcasting should be done through queued jobs so as to ensure that the response time for the application is not greatly affected.

An authentication has been introduced at the channel level for private and Websocket channels which are present.

This is shown below:

```
/*
 * Authenticate the subscription for the channel...
 */
Broadcast::channel('orders.*', function ($user,
$orderId) {

    return $user->placedOrder($orderId);
});
```

The code shows how the channel-level authentication can be done. The code will give us the orders which the user has placed.

A JavaScript package named Laravel Echo has been released, and this can be installed via NPM. This provides us with an API to help us subscribe to the channels, and listen to the server-side events in the client-side JavaScript application.

```
Echo.channel('orders.' + orderId)
  .listen('ShippingStatusUpdated', (e) => {
    console.log(e.description);
  });
```

In the above code, we are waiting for the shipping status of the order to be updated, and the code will display the "description" column of the database for that particular order, selected by its unique order id. With the Laravel Echo, we can also subscribe to the presence channels, and these will allow us to know who is listening to our channels. This is shown below:

```
Echo.join('chat.' + chatId)
  .here((users) => {
    //
  })
  .joining((user) => {
    console.log(user.name);
```

```
})
.leaving((user) => {
   console.log(user.name);
});
```

In the above code, we have subscribed to the presence channel. We have a chat

Room, and we want to know the users who are joining or leaving the chat.

The "ShouldBroadcast" Interface

Suppose a user is viewing an order. In most cases, they will be forced to refresh the page so as to see the status updates. We want to avoid this, and instead broadcast to the app as they are created. The event "ShippingStatusUpdated:" should be marked with the "ShouldBroadcast" interface. Laravel will have been instructed to broadcast the event once it has been fired. This is shown below:

```php
<?php

namespace App\Events;
use Illuminate\Queue\SerializesModels;
use Illuminate\Broadcasting\PresenceChannel;
use Illuminate\Broadcasting\PrivateChannel;
use Illuminate\Broadcasting\InteractsWithSockets;
use Illuminate\Broadcasting\Channel;
use
Illuminate\Contracts\Broadcasting\ShouldBroadcast
;

class         UpdateShippingStatus         implements
ShouldBroadcast

{
  //
}
```

The interface "ShouldBroadcast" requires the event to define some "broadcastOn" method.

The method should be tasked with returning the channels on which the events should be broadcast. An empty stub for the method has been defined on the event classes which have been generated, and we are only expected to fill in the details.

We need to make it possible for the creator of the order to be able to view the status updates, so the event will be broadcast on a private channel which has been tied on the order. This is shown below:

```
/**
 * Get the channels which the event will be broadcast on.

 * @return array
 */
public function broadcastOn()
{
    return new PrivateChannel('order.'.$this->update->order_id);
}
```

Now, we will be in a position to view the updates as they are done. The use of the "PrivateChannel" method shows that we are using a private channel for broadcasting the event on.

Authorization of Channels

Note that for users to be able to listen to the private channels, they have to be authorized to do so. The channel authorization rules can be defined in the "boot" method of the BroadcastServiceProvider. Consider the example given below, in which we want to be sure that any user who tries to listen to the private order.2 channel is actually the one who has created the order. Here is the code for the example:

```
Broadcast::channel('order.*', function ($user,
$orderId) {

   return $user->id ===
Order::findOrNew($orderId)->user_id;

});
```

Note that we have used the user_id parameter so as to know all the orders he or she has created, and then the user has been authorized to listen to those orders.

The function "channel" accepts two arguments, that is, the channel name and a callback which is expected to return either a "true" or a "false," and this shows us whether the user has been authorized to listen to the channel or not.

Note that the first argument in authorization callbacks is the user who has currently been authenticated and the other parameters will form the subsequent parameters. In the above example, we have used the wildcard character, that is, *, which shows that the ID part of the channel is a wildcard.

How to Listen for Event Broadcasts

We should learn how to listen to the event in the JavaScript application. The Laravel Echo can help us with this. We should first make use of the "first" method so as to subscribe to our private channel. The "listen" method can then be used for listening to the "ShippingStatusUpdated" event. The default setting is that the public properties of these events will have to be included on our broadcast event. This is shown below:

```
Echo.private('order.' + orderId)
  .listen('ShippingStatusUpdated', (e) => {
    console.log(e.update);
  });
```

In the above example, we are listening for any occurrence in an update of the shipping status. If the update occurs, it will be logged onto the console.

Defining Broadcast Events

We need to come up with a way of telling Laravel that a particular event needs to be broadcast. This can be done by implementing the interface "Illuminate\Contracts\Broadcasting\ShouldBroadcast" on our event class. The interface has readily been imported into the event classes which have been generated by your framework, meaning that addition of this into any events is very easy.

With the "ShouldBroadcast" interface, you are required to implement the "broadcastOn" method. The "broadcastOn" method is expected to return an array of channels or a channel to be used by the event for broadcasting on. The channels have to be created as instances of Channel, PrivateChannel, or PresenceChannel. The instances of "Channel" will present public channels which any of our users can subscribe to, while the "PresenceChannels" and "PrivateChannels" are to represent private channels which require a channel authorization. Consider the following example:

```php
<?php

namespace App\Events;

use Illuminate\Queue\SerializesModels;
use Illuminate\Broadcasting\PresenceChannel;
use Illuminate\Broadcasting\PrivateChannel;
use Illuminate\Broadcasting\InteractsWithSockets;
use Illuminate\Broadcasting\Channel;
use Illuminate\Contracts\Broadcasting\ShouldBroadcast;

class CreateServer extends Event implements ShouldBroadcast

{
  use SerializesModels;
```

```php
public $user;

/**
 * Create a new instance for the event.
 *
 * @return void
 */
public function __construct(User $user)
{
    $this->user = $user;
}

/**
 * Get the channels which our event should
 broadcast on.
 *
 * @return Channel|array
 */
public function broadcastOn()
{
    return new PrivateChannel('user.'.$this->user->id);

}
}
```

The "broadcastOn()" function has been used for definition of the channel on which the event will be broadcast. After that, you will just be expected to fire the event as normal as you do it. After firing the event, a queued job will automatically broadcast the event over the broadcast driver which you will have specified.

The Broadcast Data

After the broadcast of an event, all the public properties will be automatically serialized and then broadcast as the payload for the event, and you will be allowed to access any public data from the JavaScript description. An example is when you have an event with a single public "$user" property which has an eloquent model. In such a case, the broadcast payload for the event will be as follows:

```
{
  "user": {
    "id": 1,
    "name": "John Joel"
    ...
  }
}
```

Sometimes, you may need to have a more fine-grained control over the broadcast payload. In such a case, you may have to add the "broadcastWith" method to the event. The method will give you the data you wish to broadcast as an event payload in an array:

```
/**
 * Get the data which is to be broadcast.
 *
 * @return array
 */
public function broadcastWith()
{
    return ['id' => $this->user->id];
}
```

Note that we have used the user id, and this has been implemented within the "broadcastWith()" function. The data will then be presented in an array.

Chapter 4- Laravel Passport

Laravel 5.3 uses the Laravel Passport to make API authentication easy, and this has a full implementation of OAuth2 server for the Laravel minutes.

Passport makes it easy for us to issue access tokens via the authorization codes of OAuth2. When using the web UI, the users can be allowed to create "personal access tokens." The passport has Vue components which will serve as the starting point for the OAuth2 dashboard, and the users will be allowed to create clients, revoke the access tokens, and several others. This is shown below:

<passport-clients></passport-clients>
<passport-authorized-clients></passport-authorized-clients>

<passport-personal-access-tokens></passport-personal-access-tokens>

The content should be added between the above tags. Note the use of a forward slash "/" which signifies closing of the token. If you don't need to use the Vue components, you can use the frontend dashboard for management of the clients and the access tokens. Passport provides us with a simple JSON API which can be used together with any JavaScript framework one chooses.

The Passport also makes it easy for us to define the scope for access tokens which the app which consumes the API may request. This is shown below:

Passport::tokensCan([
  'place-orders' => 'Place a new order',
  'check-status' => 'Check the status of order',
]);

Passport also has a middleware which can be used for verification of the request which has been authenticated by the access token so as to ensure that it has the necessary scopes for the token. This is demonstrated below:

```
Route::get('/orders/{order}/status', function (Order $order) {

    // Our Access token is having the "check-status" scope...

})->middleware('scope:check-status');
```

Search

The Laravel Scout provides us with a simple and driver-based solution for addition of full-text search to the Eloquent models. By use of model servers, Scout can automatically keep the search indexes in sync with the Eloquent records. Currently, the Scout comes with the Angolia driver, but it easy for you to write your own driver, and you can easily extend it to the search implementations.

For a model to be made searchable, we just have to add the "searchable" attribute to it. This is shown below:

```php
<?php

namespace App;

use Laravel\Scout\Searchable;
use Illuminate\Database\Eloquent\Model;

class Message extends Model
{
    use Searchable;
}
```

The "searchable" property has been implemented using the "use" keyword.

Once the trait has been added to the model, the information will then be kept in sync with the search indexes, simply by the saving of the model.

```php
$order = new Order;
// ...
$order->save();
```

Note that saving of the model has been done by use of the "save()" method.

After indexing of the models, it will be easy for you to carry out full-text searches across the models. The search results can also be displayed in pages, and this can be implemented as follows:

return Order::search('Boss Worker')->get();

return Order::search('Boss Worker')->where('user_id', 1)->paginate();

In the above case, the search term is "Boss Worker," and the id of the user should be 1.

Batch Import

Suppose you want to install the Scout into a project, and there are some database records which you need to import into the search driver. Scout provides us with the "import" Artisan command which one can use to import the existing records into the search indexes. This is demonstrated below:

php artisan scout:import "App\Post"

How to Add Records

After addition of the "Laravel\Scout\Searchable" trait to the model, we use the "save()" method for adding it to the search index as we did previously.

It is also possible for this to be done via a query. The query can be used for the addition of a collection of models to the search index via the Eloquent query. With the "searchable" method, the query results will be put into chunks, and the records will be added to the search index. If the Scout has been configured to use queues, all the chinks will be added to the background by the queue workers. This is shown below:

// Add via an Eloquent query...

```
App\Order::where('cost', '>', 50)->searchable();
```

```
// Records can also be added via relationships...
$user->orders()->searchable();
```

```
// Records may also be added via collections...
$orders->searchable();
```

Note that in the first case, we have used an eloquent query, and the "searchable()" method will be applied where the cost is greater than 50. In the second case, the relationship between the user and the order has been used for this.

The "searchable" method can be seen as an upsert operation. This means that if the model record is in the index, then it will have to be updated. If it is not available in the search index, then it will have to be added to the index.

Sometimes, you may be in need of updating the searchable method. You just have to update the properties of the model instance, and then apply the "save" method on the model. With Socut, the changes will be automatically applied to the database. Consider the following example:

```
$order = App\Order::find(2);
```

```
// Update your order...
```

```
$order->save();
```

Note that the "save()" method has been created after the order has been updated.

Removal of Records

If you need to remove a record from the index, you just have to delete the model from the database. However, this cannot be applied to soft completed models.

```
$order = App\Order::find(1);
```

```
$order->delete();
```

If you want to delete the record and then retrieve the model, the "unsearchable" method can be used on some instance of Eloquent query or a collection. This is shown below:

```
// Remove record via an Eloquent query...
App\Order::where('cost', '>', 50)->unsearchable();
```

```
// It can also be removed via relationships...
$user->orders()->unsearchable();
```

```
// It can also be removed via collections...
$orders->unsearchable();
```

Pausing Indexing

Sometimes, you may need to perform a batch of Eloquent operations on a model with no need to perform a sync of the model data to the search index. The "withoutSyncingToSearch" can help us implement this. The method will accept only a single callback, and this will have to be executed immediately. Any model operations to occur within a callback won't be synced to the index of the model. This is shown below:

```
App\Order::withoutSyncingToSearch(function () {
    // Perform the model actions...
});
```

The actions on the model should be done within the function.

Searching

You may need to search for a model by use of the "search" method. The method will accept a single string, and this will be used for searching for the model. The "get" method can then be chained onto your search query so as to retrieve the Eloquent models which have matched the query. This is shown below:

$orders = App\Order::search('Boss Worker')->get();

In our example, the search term is "Boss Worker," and as you can see, it has been passed as the argument to the "search" method.

Remember that the search will return a collection of some Eloquent models, meaning that you can directly return the results from a route or a controller, and these will be automatically converted into a controller. This is shown below:

use Illuminate\Http\Request;

Route::get('/search', function (Request $request) {
**   return   App\Order::search($request->search)->get();**

});

Chapter 5- Mailable Objects

Laravel has a clean and simple API which has drivers for Mailgun, SMTP, Amazon SES, SparkPost, sendmail, and the PHP mail function, and these can help to easily send your mail via a local or cloud based service you choose.

Drivers which are based on APIs are usually easy and faster to use compared to the SMTP servers. It will be good for you to use one of such drivers if it is possible. All API drivers need the Guzzle HTTP library, and we can install this via the composer package manager. The following command can be used for this purpose:

composer require guzzlehttp/guzzle

Mailgun Driver

For you to use the Mailgun driver, you should first install the Guzzle HTTP library, and the driver option in the configuration file named "config/mail.php" should be set to "mailgun." Next, you have to check whether your configuration file "config/services.php" has the options given below:

```
'mailgun' => [
  'domain' => 'mailgun-domain',
  'secret' => 'mailgun-key',
],
```

SparkPost Driver

For you to use this driver, you should first install the Guzzle, and the "driver" option in the "config/mail.php" configuration file should be set to "sparkpost." The "config/services.php" should then be checked for the options given below:

```
'sparkpost' => [
```

```
    'secret' => 'sparkpost-key',
],
```

SES Driver

For this driver to be used, the Amazon AWS SDK for PHP should first be installed. To install this, just add the line given below to the "require" section of the "composer.json" file and then the "composer update" command executed:

"aws/aws-sdk-php": "~3.0"

You should then set the "driver" option in the file "config/mail.php" to "ses," and then check the "config/services.php" configuration file for the following options:

```
'ses' => [
    'key' => 'ses-key',
    'secret' => 'ses-secret',
    'region' => 'ses-region',  // e.g. us-east-1
],
```

How to Generate Mailables

In Laravel, any email which is sent by the application has to be represented as a "mailable" class. Such classes are represented in the directory named "app/Mail." This directory is automatically created once you execute the "make:mail" method for the first time.

php artisan make:mail OrderShipped

That is how the command is executed.

How to Write Mailables

The configuration of the mailable class is done with the "build" method. A number of methods can be called within the above method and these include from, subject, view, and attach methods, and these will help you configure how the email will be sent.

Sender Configuration

There are a number of methods which can be used for configuration of the sender. Let us discuss these.

The "from" method

The email should specify the person from whom it originates. This can be done by use of the "from" method within the "build" method. Consider the following example:

```
/**
 * Build your message.
 *
 * @return $this
 */
public function build()
{
    return $this->from('name@domain.com')
        ->view('emails.orders.shipped');
}
```

The Global "from" Address

Such an address should only be used only when there is not another "from" address which has been specified in the mailable class. This is shown below:

```
'from' => ['address' => 'name@domain.com', 'name'
=> 'Application Name'],
```

Plain Text Mails

Sometimes, you may need to define a plain text version for your email. In such a case, you can accomplish that by the use of the "text" method. The method will accept a name for a template which will then be used for the purpose of rendering the content for the mail. Feel free to create both Plain-text and HTML versions for any of your messages. This is demonstrated below:

```
/**
 * Building the message.
 *
 * @return $this
 */
public function build()
{
    return $this->view('emails.orders.shipped')
        ->text('emails.orders.shipped_plain');
}
```

Conclusion

We have come to the end of this guide. My hope is that you have learned how to use the Laravel Framework. This framework makes development of apps very exciting and enjoyable. In the development of web applications, there are must-implement features.

These are the common features which are desirable in almost all web applications. Examples of such include sessions, user authentication, routing, and caching. So far, you must have discovered that Laravel makes development a bit easy and quicker with no interfering or decreasing the functionality of the app.

 It is a very powerful web framework, yet very accessible, and one can use it for the development of robust web applications.

The framework has a superb migration system, a good control container, and a unit testing support which is tightly integrated.

The framework gives you all the necessary tools you need for the development of web applications.

www.ingramcontent.com/pod-product-compliance
Lightning Source LLC
Chambersburg PA
CBHW070900070326
40690CB00009B/1931